The Power
of
Strategic Partnering

The Master Management Series

William F. Christopher
Editor-in-Chief

3

The Power
of
Strategic Partnering

Eberhard E. Scheuing

PRODUCTIVITY PRESS

Portland, Oregon

Volume 3 of the *Management Master Series*.
William F. Christopher, Editor-in-Chief
Copyright © 1994 by Productivity Press, Inc.

Productivity Press
P.O. Box 13390
Portland OR 97213-0390
United States of America
Telephone: 503-235-0600
Telefax: 503-235-0909

ISBN: 1-56327-065-X

Book design by William Stanton
Composition by Rohani Design
Printed and bound by BookCrafters in the United States of America

Library of Congress Cataloging-in-Publication Data

Scheuing, Eberhard E. (Eberhard Eugen), 1939–
    The power of strategic partnering / Eberhard E. Schueing.
        p.   cm. -- (Management master series ; v. 3)
    Includes bibliographical references.
    ISBN 1-56327-065-X
    1. Strategic alliances (Business) 2. Corporate planning.
    3. Contracting out. 4. Partnership. I. Title. II. Series.
    HD69.S8S33   1994
    658'.044--dc20   94-27921
                                                                            CIP

98 97 96 95   10 9 8 7 6 5 4 3 2

—CONTENTS—

PUBLISHER'S MESSAGE

The *Management Master Series* was designed to discover and disseminate to you the world's best concepts, principles, and current practices in excellent management. We present this information in a concise and easy-to-use format to provide you with the tools and techniques you need to stay abreast of this rapidly accelerating world of ideas.

World class competitiveness requires managers today to be thoroughly informed about how and what other internationally successful managers are doing. What works? What doesn't? and Why?

Management is often considered a "neglected art." It is not possible to know how to manage before you are made a manager. But once you become a manager you are expected to know how to manage and to do it well, right from the start.

One result of this neglect in management training has been managers who rely on control rather than creativity. Certainly, managers in this century have shown a distinct neglect of workers as creative human beings. The idea that employees are an organization's most valuable asset is still very new. How managers can inspire and direct the creativity and intelligence of everyone involved in the work of an organization has only begun to emerge.

Perhaps if we consider management as a "science" the task of learning how to manage well will be easier. A scientist begins with an hypothesis and then runs experiments to observe whether the hypothesis is correct. Scientists depend on detailed notes about the experiment—the timing, the ingredients, the amounts—and carefully record all results as they test new hypotheses. Certain things come to be known by this method; for instance, that water always consists of one part oxygen and two parts hydrogen.

We as managers must learn from our experience and from the experience of others. The scientific approach provides a model for learning. Science begins with vision and desired outcomes, and achieves its purpose through observation, experiment, and analysis of precisely recorded results. And then what is newly discovered is shared so that each person's research will build on the work of others.

Our organizations, however, rarely provide the time for learning or experimentation. As a manager, you need information from those who have already experimented and learned and recorded their results. You need it in brief, clear, and detailed form so that you can apply it immediately.

It is our purpose to help you confront the difficult task of managing in these turbulent times. As the shape of leadership changes, the *Management Master Series* will continue to bring you the best learning available to support your own increasing artistry in the evolving science of management.

We at Productivity Press are grateful to William F. Christopher and our staff of editors who have searched out those masters with the knowledge, experience, and ability to write concisely and completely on excellence in management practice. We wish also to thank the individual volume authors; Cheryl Rosen and Diane Asay, project managers; Julie Zinkus, manuscript editor; Karen Jones, managing editor; Lisa Hoberg, Mary Junewick, and Julie Hankin, editorial support; Bill Stanton, design and production management; Susan Swanson, production coordination; Rohani Design, composition.

Norman Bodek
Publisher

INTRODUCTION

We live in a fast-paced world where the risks of going it alone are growing by the minute. Powerful economic forces are reshaping companies, industries, and countries. Enlightened leaders recognize the need to join forces with others for mutual benefit. They configure continuously evolving networks of resources engaged in joint value creation. The members of these networks are lean and flexible organizations committed to continuous improvement. They are linked by common interests and the opportunity to leverage their strengths. They continually strengthen their relationships because of the substantial rewards produced by the resulting synergy.

1

THE DYNAMICS OF TURBULENCE

The pace of change in our society and economy is steadily accelerating. Rather than being evolutionary and natural, it tends to be revolutionary and disruptive. Traditional paradigms are unable to cope with the scope and violence of change. Radical rethinking and restructuring of processes, organizations, and relationships is essential for survival and growth in a turbulent world.

FORCES DRIVING CHANGE

In an increasingly interdependent world, no company, industry, or even country can remain an island unto itself. Faced with seemingly limitless opportunities and challenges but limited resources of their own, modern organizations seek additional leverage by joining forces with others. Below is a list of the powerful forces that are reshaping the way we do business on a global basis.

Forces Driving Change

- Technological evolution and competitive threats
- Market opportunities and capital requirements
- Cost pressures and resource constraints
- Quality requirements and outsourcing strategies

Technological Evolution and Competitive Threats

Technological evolution is so rapid and costly that it often requires joint efforts. Corning Incorporated has elevated joint venturing to the level of an art, teaming up with such industry leaders as Dow Chemical in the United States, Siemens in Germany, and Asahi Glass in Japan. The U.S. government is recognizing the need for even the largest companies in an industry to cooperate in order to advance the state of the art. It has thus granted antitrust exemptions and permitted, or even encouraged, research jointly sponsored by *competitors*, provided that both costs and results are shared. In the semiconductor industry, Sematech has obtained funding and participation from such companies as AT&T and IBM, who otherwise continue to compete vigorously. Similarly, the Big Three automobile companies are cooperating in an effort to develop new materials to achieve greater fuel efficiency.

Market Opportunities and Capital Requirements

In the newly deregulated European skies, competitive threats from U.S.-based carriers are so strong that all of the European national flag carriers are seeking cross-border alliances to counteract the onslaught. Both the *market opportunities* and *capital requirements* in the converging telecom/cable markets are so vast—domestically as well as internationally—that even large players like U.S. West and Time-Warner can see considerable merit in combining their strengths.

Cost Pressures and Resource Constraints

The relentless pressure of global competition produces similarly unending *cost pressures* to keep providing goods and/or services at low cost. This quest is not likely to succeed without the active and continuing support and participation of like-minded partners. Companies like Ford and Xerox enter into multiyear agreements with selected suppliers that set specific annual savings targets. Their three-year contracts specify that the suppliers must pass on cost savings of 5 percent per year for a total reduction of 15 percent over the contract term. If the suppliers are unable to achieve such savings on their own, their customer partners provide trained personnel to assist in this effort. Honda of America makes engineers available to help its 330 suppliers improve quality and productivity. They form teams with supplier technical personnel that typically produce savings of 50 percent, shared equally with the suppliers. Chrysler successfully enlisted its suppliers' cooperation in its SCORE (Supplier Cost Reduction Effort) program. Since its initiation, Chrysler has received more than 4,600 cost-saving suggestions for a total savings of $235 million. Motorola and Toyota conduct training programs for their suppliers to help them in their quality management and cost reduction efforts.

Limited resources—physical, financial, and/or human—also cause many companies to augment their bases by reaching out and seeking strength in numbers. Airbus Industrie is an international consortium of French, British, and German companies that has managed to wean itself from initial government subsidies and compete effectively against American airframe manufacturers.

Quality Requirements and Outsourcing Strategies

The need to *continuously improve product quality* also requires companies to team up with key suppliers. Cadbury Beverages calls the members of this core group its Valued Partners and works closely with them to maintain its competitive edge. As companies develop a better understanding of their core competencies and decide to concentrate on them, *outsourcing* of complementary activities becomes an increasingly attractive opportunity. This has long been a practice in the garment industry where fashion leaders concentrate on designing and marketing, but outsource actual production to independent suppliers.

MANAGING VALUE CREATION

Value is the relationship between performance and cost:

$$\text{Value} = \frac{\text{Performance}}{\text{Cost}}$$

This relationship exists in the minds of customers. *Customers* are the persons or units who depend on a supplier's performance for the success of their own efforts. To customers, value is perceived performance as related to the cost of obtaining it from suppliers. *Suppliers* are persons or units who enable customers to succeed in their efforts.

Establishing Value Chains

As suppliers and customers create and transfer value in their interactions, they become links in a value chain that extends from a supplier's supplier to a company's external customer. Figure 1 illustrates this situation.

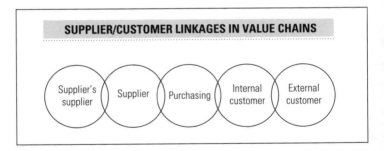

Figure 1. Supplier/Customer Linkages in Value Chains

Figure 1 shows that the value chain is also a chain of dependency. What the external customer receives depends not only on what the internal customer/supplier does, but also on what earlier links in the chain contributed to it. In fact, every downstream link is affected by the contributions and output of earlier links. As each link adds its own contribution, a total value package is created in successive stages. This package is designed and intended to satisfy the requirements of the ultimate customer in the chain.

To achieve this goal and create lasting competitive advantage in the process, a company must proactively manage the interactions between the links of the value chain. This requires a comprehensive strategy that leverages the strengths of the individual links for maximum joint advantage.

Managing Value Chains

Purchasing represents a company's interface with its supplier base. Therefore, purchasing professionals must carefully select suppliers who can bring genuine value to the company. They must also monitor and manage supplier performance to ensure that suppliers continually deliver and enhance this value. The Tennant Company, a Midwestern manufacturer of motorized floor sweepers, exemplifies best practices in value-chain management. Its supplier management teams, led by purchasers, thoroughly screen and evaluate suppliers on an ongoing basis. They provide suppliers with continuous feedback on how well they meet Tennant's requirements and how they can improve performance further.

Tennant's Supplier Satisfaction Rating form consists of three major sections. In sections I and II, suppliers can earn one of four ratings: excellent, good, average, or poor. Section I, General Impression, poses two questions:

- How well does this supplier meet Tennant's quality expectations?

- How well do they meet our expectations in the following areas? (11 areas, ranging from product reliability to top management involvement.)

Section II, Customer Satisfaction, contains four questions:

- How well does sales representation meet our expectations? (7 areas, ranging from frequency of contact to accessibility.)

- How well do they meet our expectations on purchase orders and delivery? (6 areas, ranging from meet promise dates to packaging.)

- How well do they meet our engineering support expectations? (7 areas, ranging from knowledge of our applications to overall responsiveness.)

- How well does this supplier work with us in containing costs? (8 areas, ranging from controls price increases to performance vs. inflation.)

Section III presents the broad question:

- What other areas do we need to address to mutually improve our customer/supplier relationship?

TOWARD NETWORKS OF RELATIONSHIPS

It quickly becomes evident that the concept of a linear value chain is a simplification. It does help to highlight the dependence of downstream outputs on upstream inputs. It fails, however, to reflect that actual inputs from multiple sources interact in complex ways to produce the varied outputs that different customers value. This shortcoming of the value-chain concept leads to the insight that cutting-edge organizations are really the hubs of networks of relationships.

Core Competency

In a highly volatile environment, companies must steadily reexamine their missions and related core competencies. A *core competency* is a unique advantage that sets a company apart from its competition and is thus at the very heart of its mission and distinctiveness. For strategic reasons, core competencies must be retained in-house, because outsourcing them would cut into the very essence of a company's uniqueness and vision of itself. All other functions and components, however, can—and perhaps should—be outsourced to other organizations who can provide them better and perhaps less expensively.

Vertically integrated corporations who supply themselves are a thing of the past. No company can be excellent in every part of its operations. In fact, in these increasingly competitive times, there is a penalty to pay for making everything in-house, including both goods and services. General Motors is among the major corporations who have discovered that outside suppliers can be more efficient than their own parts-making operations. Accordingly, the company is aggressively selling off many of its parts-making plants. On the other hand, its Electronic Data Systems unit, a former independent service supplier that GM acquired from Ross Perot in the '80s, has been a solid money-maker. This unit has continued to grow in the face of vigorous global competition precisely because it offers a unique core competency. Moreover, its parent corporation is just one of its clients. EDS snatched a $1.48 billion contract to run the computers of the British tax agency from IBM and other rivals.

Reengineering the Corporation

The trend to reexamine corporate structures and sourcing arrangements has been called *reengineering* or *reinventing the corporation*. Leading organizations have discovered that this effort must be ongoing. They must continually analyze operational processes to determine how to streamline them. They must eliminate activities or steps that do not add value, and increase efficiency by identifying the best source for specific process components. Almost inevitably, this strategic analysis of the value creation process results in a reconfiguration of both the process itself and the sources of its components. As Figure 2 illustrates, the corporate paradigm for the twenty-first century is a streamlined organization that functions as the intelligent hub of a network of relationships.

The network of partnerships can be extended to other areas of opportunity, as Figure 3 shows. Organizations can form research and development (R&D) partnerships to discover and develop new technology that one or both partners can then market. They can create new business or new market partner-

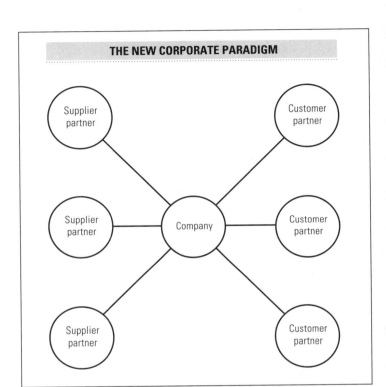

Figure 2. The New Corporate Paradigm

ships to combine resources for the development of new markets. Through linkages with international partners, companies can seize business opportunities in other countries. Creative leaders can use the partnering process as a powerful engine for improvement and growth.

Some have labeled this emerging arrangement a *virtual corporation*. It involves a highly flexible network of independent organizations who combine their core competencies in creative ways to respond to and capitalize on rapidly evolving capabilities and opportunities. Virtual corporations possess the following key attributes:

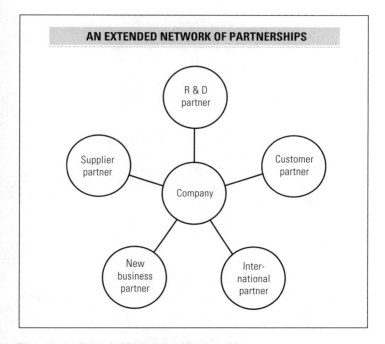

AN EXTENDED NETWORK OF PARTNERSHIPS

R & D partner

Supplier partner

Company

Customer partner

New business partner

Inter- national partner

Figure 3. An Extended Network of Partnerships

- *Advanced information technology:* They have internal and external databases, high-speed information network linkages, and electronic data interchange (EDI) with partners.

- *Flexibility:* Impermanence of their own structures allows them to link with and de-link from partners as opportunities arise and fade.

- *Dependence:* No longer self-contained and autonomous, virtual corporations cannot function without their partners who contribute vital inputs to the network.

- *Borderless linkages:* National boundaries as well as traditional distinctions between suppliers, competitors, and customers lose meaning as networks synergistically combine inputs into optimum outputs.

- *Excellence:* The single most powerful force in virtual corporations is the unrelenting commitment to excellence, which draws on the unique competencies of several organizations for world-class outputs.

This network of expert resources is likely to be composed of organizations in diverse geographic locations. It is closely linked, however, by strong corporate commitment and state-of-the-art information technology to ensure smooth cooperation and coordination. The network can be successful only if it is composed of learning organizations. These organizations continually create and acquire new knowledge and capabilities. As a result, they continuously improve their processes and performance.

The resulting configuration has been referred to as a *value constellation.* It involves a radical rethinking of the relative roles and responsibilities of customers and suppliers in the process of value creation. IKEA, the world's largest furniture retailer, has built its success on a revolutionary system that combines a global network of suppliers with an expanded participation of customers in the process of value creation. To offer high-quality, low-cost furniture to consumers all over the world, IKEA designs its own products and outsources their production to 1800 suppliers in more than 50 countries. IKEA carefully manages its relationships with them and assists them in many details of their daily operations. Defying conventional logic, IKEA sells furniture in kit form in large self-service warehouse stores. Several tasks that furniture manufacturers and retailers usually perform, such as assembly and delivery, are transferred to consumers, who thus become partial co-producers in the value creation process.

2

THE PARTNERING IMPERATIVE

In a global marketplace characterized by turbulent change and aggressive competition, no organization, regardless of size, can afford to go it alone any more. Driven by forces beyond their control, companies around the world are entering into strategic alliances to bolster their strengths and overcome their weaknesses. Having explored their options, they enter into various kinds of commitments that they select from a continuum of possible partnering arrangements. Entering into this process of cooperation involves a series of steps that lead to smoothly functioning linkages. To ensure the best possible arrangements, both the risks and benefits of partnering must be examined and managed carefully.

PARTNERING OPTIONS

Leaders who understand the importance of strategic partnering can choose from a number of options they can use separately or, better yet, in conjunction with each other. Figure 4 shows these alternative courses of action.

The strategic partnering matrix highlights the powerful and versatile tool of partnering that companies can use with internal and/or external partners in a horizontal or vertical manner. Figure 4 illustrates this matrix by looking at the supply side of the value chain. In this context, the term internal partnering refers to joint efforts that take place among col-

	Type Direction	Internal partnering	External partnering
STRATEGIC PARTNERING MATRIX **(SUPPLIER OR INPUT SIDE)**			
Horizontal partnering		Pooled purchasing	Cooperative purchasing
Vertical partnering		Sourcing teams	Supplier partnering

Figure 4. Strategic Partnering Matrix (Supplier or Input Side)

leagues within the same corporate family. In contrast, external partnering describes alliances between independent firms. The expression horizontal partnering reflects cooperation between people or organizations at the same position in the value chain. Conversely, vertical partnering takes place between players in different positions on the value chain.

Pooled Purchasing

Purchasers of similar or identical products that different units of the same firm use can work together meaningfully and beneficially in company-wide commodity councils. Pooled purchasing allows them to combine their separate purchasing volumes for increased leverage. Toward this end, they must agree on common specifications and manage supplier relations jointly. While this kind of intracorporate cooperation makes a great deal of sense to disinterested observers, it is far from common practice in many large corporations. In one global beverage company, for instance, subsidiaries in different countries failed to agree on a common bottle cap. Each unit claimed that its choice was superior. Such internecine differences are all too frequent. Turfism and the not-invented-here syndrome often prevent cooperation for the common good.

Sourcing Teams

Curiously, it is typically much easier to achieve vertical cooperation within an organization. Colleagues in different functions, whose responsibilities are interrelated, widely accept and recognize the necessity and benefits of teamwork. Sourcing teams are groups composed of representatives from relevant functions who jointly manage supplier relations for selected products. Depending on the needs of the particular situation, the purchaser, as process owner, can draw on the expertise of engineering, quality assurance, production/operations, finance/accounting, the internal customer unit, and the legal department. The team members join forces on supplier plant visits, selection, performance evaluation, and support.

Cooperative Purchasing

Cooperative purchasing combines the purchasing volumes of several independent organizations for increased leverage. Historically, it has taken place mainly in the form of purchasing cooperatives and purchasing consortia.

PURCHASING COOPERATIVES

A *purchasing cooperative* is a group of nonprofit organizations or government agencies who band together to achieve greater efficiency in procuring selected commodities that they all require in substantial volumes. Such cooperatives have a long history in the institutional and public sectors. They involve the formation of a separate nonprofit organization that coordinates and administers the purchasing process for the member organizations who pay annual dues. Affiliated suppliers pay fees to the central organization. The Joint Purchasing Corporation of New York has long served as the buying arm of a number of nonprofit hospitals for selected commodities.

PURCHASING CONSORTIUM

A purchasing consortium, on the other hand, is a small, informal group of independent business firms who jointly buy selected products. Rather than forming a separate legal entity for this endeavor, the team members cooperate informally and share the work. In further contrast to a cooperative, the member firms do not pay any dues, but participate actively in the sourcing process. To alleviate potential antitrust challenges, participating firms tend to represent different industries. Interestingly, global firms with substantial purchasing volumes of their own can nonetheless benefit greatly from consortium purchasing.

Supplier Partnering

The final option illustrated in Figure 4 is *supplier partnering,* which is the strategic establishment, systematic maintenance, and proactive enhancement of close, mutually beneficial, long-term business relationships with a limited number of carefully selected suppliers. These characteristics are highlighted in the list below.

Key Aspects of Supplier Partnering

• Strategic	-	Corporate philosophy
• Systematic	-	Organized
• Proactive	-	Unsolicited initiative
• Close	-	Continuous dialog
• Mutually beneficial	-	Win-win situation
• Business	-	Arms-length
• Limited number	-	Supplier team
• Suppliers	-	External resources

Supplier partnering is a strategic commitment between two independent firms that transcends the realm of purchasing and requires a supportive corporate philosophy. To be effective, the partners need to execute it in an organized fashion, based on continuous improvements that either partner may initiate. Both sides share the benefits. Although close cooperation is necessary, the relationships must remain at arms length.

Supplier partnering can only be carried out with a manageable number of suppliers. Therefore, most companies that

engage in supplier partnering progressively downsize their supplier bases. Xerox attacked this task most aggressively, reducing
its list of active suppliers from 5,000 to 500 within less than
two years. Ford trimmed its supplier pool from 1,800 to 1,000
and plans further reductions to a target of 300. Companies sim-
ply find it impossible to manage thousands of suppliers on an
ongoing basis. That is a key reason why they focus their ener-
gies on working with a chosen few who are often single sources
for given products.

Customer Partnering

Figure 4 looked at the supply or input side of the value
chain. Figure 5 shows a comparable matrix for the customer or
output side.

STRATEGIC PARTNERING MATRIX (CUSTOMER OR OUTPUT SIDE)		
Type / Direction	Internal partnering	External partnering
Horizontal partnering	National account marketing	Cooperative marketing
Vertical partnering	Marketing teams	Customer partnering

Figure 5. Strategic Partnering Matrix (Customer or Output Side)

INTERNAL PARTNERING

Horizontal internal partnering involves *national account
marketing*, in which a company centrally coordinates and
manages the marketing efforts of different corporate units that
are directed toward the same customer.

Vertical internal partnering occurs in the form of marketing teams that pull together talent from the different functions

that serve a customer. These include design engineering, pro-
duction/operations, logistics, customer service, and billing.

EXTERNAL PARTNERING

Horizontal external partnering takes the form of *cooperative
marketing* in which independent organizations market their
products jointly. This has long been a practice in the agricultural
sector. Sunkist and Ocean Spray are brands that growers' cooperatives own and market.

The final cell of *customer partnering* is the mirror image of
supplier partnering, seen and managed from the supplier's perspective.

THE PARTNERING CONTINUUM

Figure 6 depicts the range of potential cooperative
arrangements.

THE PARTNERING CONTINUUM

| Informal cooperation | Formal agreement | Minority investment | Joint venture |

Figure 6. The Partnering Continuum

Informal Cooperation

Informal cooperation involves a joint effort that does not
require a new organization or a written contract. This kind of
arrangement is, of course, typical for internal partnering because
it takes place within the same corporate family and does not
involve linkages between independent organizations. Its major

advantage is flexibility. Its major disadvantage is a lack of clear accountability and commitment.

Formal Agreement

A *formal agreement* is a negotiated, written contract that two or more parties sign, that explicitly spells out the respective rights and obligations of the players involved. It is an appropriate and necessary safeguard when independent organizations make long-term commitments to each other. Such agreements are accordingly common in external partnering arrangements, both horizontal and vertical. Their major benefit is a detailed understanding of the nature of the commitment. Their major drawback is the inherent rigidity of formal agreements.

Minority Investment

A *minority investment* is an equity investment in an independent company that represents less than a controlling interest; that is, less than 51 percent of the shareholders' equity in this firm. It certainly means "putting money where one's mouth is." Ford owns 25 percent of Mazda and 40 percent of Exel, the supplier of windows for the vehicles it makes. This level of commitment goes beyond an arms-length linkage and provides critical equity financing that represents patient capital and offers financial stability.

Joint Venture

In a *joint venture*, two corporations closely link their fortunes by forming a new legal entity in which they both invest capital (usually 50/50) and which they thus jointly own. The principal reasons for this kind of strategic partnering are market opportunities and complementary strengths of the parent organizations. Historically, such arrangements were useful vehicles for European fiber manufacturers to enter the American market. Typically, the European partner brought technology, and the American partner brought market access to the joint venture. Mobay, a joint venture formed by Monsanto and

Bayer, is an example of this pattern. Since the parent organizations often remain competitors in the world marketplace, many of these joint ventures eventually end when, due to diverging philosophies, one partner buys out the other's interest.

In a similar vein, joint ventures remain the vehicle of choice for international market entry in countries where the law does not permit wholly owned subsidiaries. Here, teaming up with a well-established national company in a joint venture not only satisfies the law, but also provides valuable local identity. Corning Incorporated has used the powerful vehicle of joint venturing masterfully in 19 domestic and international alliances that provide it with unequaled access to talent, markets, and capital.

THE PARTNERING PROCESS

The process of strategic partnering evolves through four major stages. Each stage consists of three steps. Figure 7 depicts this process.

Realization

The first stage, *realization*, involves recognizing that the traditional pattern of aloofness is no longer in the best interests of the organization.

1. Management sees a *need* to move from disparate transactions with many counterparts to long-term relationships with few partners.

2 Management *decides* to significantly reduce both the number of individual transactions and the number of players involved.

3. Management *selects* the members they want to be part of this inner circle of partners.

Step 3 is necessary and ultimately rewarding, but it can also be quite painful for two reasons: It signifies a radically new way of doing business, and it means saying good-bye to a lot of old acquaintances. All change inflicts pain, and parting with the

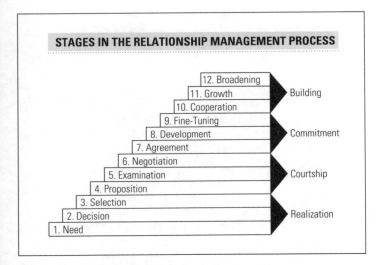

Figure 7. Stages in the Relationship Management Process

"good old days" of multiple sourcing or mass marketing requires a significant change in attitude. Telling long-time business contacts that they did not "make the cut" is a gut-wrenching experience. Many of them had been good, if unexciting, customers or suppliers for quite some time. Understandably, they resent being cut off. But the harsh realities of a turbulent marketplace no longer permit the luxury of trying to be everything to everybody. Rather, they dictate focusing and leveraging.

Because the selection and its results are inevitably painful, companies may want to involve all candidates in the process and offer them a chance to influence the outcome. When Xerox committed radical surgery on its supplier base, it invited *informed consent* by conveying to all of its suppliers the nature of and rationale for its strategic decision, then encouraging them to offer reasons why they should be among the chosen few. Similarly, companies should offer customers and employees likely to be affected by streamlining a chance to influence the outcome. They may be willing to make substantial commitments to invest in, or even acquire, the operations slated for closure or sale. There are examples of successful buyouts by customers, employees, and/or management or partial employee ownership in return for labor concessions or givebacks.

Courtship

After selecting the prospective partners, the company enters the *courtship* stage. The prime objective of this stage is to get prospects to commit to the partnering concept. It could thus be compared to a "mating dance."

4. The company initiates a *proposition*, which is essentially a marketing effort. It is designed to obtain prospect buy-in to both the concept of partnering and the specific configuration. Presented with great enthusiasm and conviction, it is likely to elicit a guarded, though positive, response from the prospect's management.

5. Before committing itself to a close cooperation for the longer term, the prospective partner *examines* the impact of such a commitment on its other working relationships.

6. Upon completion of this examination, if the prospective partner is interested, both parties *negotiate* the dimensions of this potential commitment in detail. As this discussion clarifies points and resolves differences, the parties move closer to agreement.

Commitment

The third stage, *commitment,* cements the relationship between the parties and provides the transition to genuine partnering.

7. The parties reach an *agreement* and inaugurate the new partnering relationship. Having moved beyond casual interaction, this step truly represents a turning point because it requires real commitment and an irreversible change of course.

Such a quantum leap may well warrant senior-level involvement as it does at Cadbury Beverages. They sign and countersign a Valued Partner agreement with a key supplier at the Chief Executive level. This signifies the total commitment of both organizations.

8. Next, the partners *develop* operational coordination, particularly in the form of electronic linkages and frequent personal interaction.

9. The partners pilot and *fine-tune* the linkages and work out the bugs to ensure smooth coordination.

Building

The commitment effort bears fruit in the *building* stage, during which the partners continually implement the newly formed partnering arrangement.

10. The partners *cooperate* daily, generating the fruits that the realization stage anticipated.

11. The momentum of this joint effort pays off in the form of volume and profit *growth* for both partners. This beneficial outcome, in turn, is likely to encourage discussions in step 12.

12. As a result of this beneficial outcome, the partners discuss *broadening* the partnering relationship to include other products and/or services.

In the process of selecting partners, a substantial number of factors need to be given due consideration. Figure 8 lists such factors.

Designed to be generic in nature, these considerations in partner selection generally prove useful in relationships between independent firms. A few do not apply readily to internal partnering. The criteria essentially indicate the desirability of long-term linkages with specific prospects. They also suggest discussions and "prenuptial agreements" about respective rights and obligations before anyone makes a commit-

---

CONSIDERATIONS IN PARTNER SELECTION

1. Past quality and delivery performance
2. Cost
3. Capacity
4. Capabilities
5. Responsiveness and promptness in problem resolution
6. Management abilities and philosophy
7. Financial performance and stability
8. Professionalism, teamwork, and compatibility
9. Exclusivity, confidentiality, security, and vulnerability
10. Ownership of patents and intellectual property rights
11. Relative size, power, and control
12. Required investment
13. Economic rewards
14. Interdependence
15. Arm's-length relationship
16. Form of interaction
17. Flexibility and willingness to change
18. Ability to serve global needs

Figure 8. Considerations in Partner Selection

ment. And they highlight the necessity of examining the possibility of terminating the partnering arrangement and the consequences of such an action for the parties involved.

RISKS AND BENEFITS OF PARTNERING

Strategic partnering, like any other human endeavor, involves both challenges and opportunities. Its risks have to be carefully weighed against its prospective benefits to arrive at the best solution. We will now explore both sides of the partnering coin.

Potential Risks of Strategic Partnering

It would be foolhardy not to realize or admit that strategic partnering carries a number of risks. A list of these potential risks follows.

Risks of Partnering

- Complacency
- Coziness
- Clouded judgment
- Sloppiness

- Conflict of interest
- Dependence
- Vulnerability
- Switching costs

COMPLACENCY AND CONFLICT OF INTEREST

Clearly, one of the great risks of strategic partnering is taking each other for granted and feeling that no effort is required to maintain or build the relationship. Such *complacency* is ill-placed in today's fast-paced and highly competitive environment where change is the only constant. The situation gets worse when the loyalties of the players are challenged. They may run into *conflicts of interest* that compel them to put their personal interests ahead of their responsibility to their employers. The close working relationships in strategic partnering can create such ethical dilemmas. It is therefore advisable, particularly in external partnering, that a firm not only create and communicate a code of conduct for its own employees, but also that they agree on and spell out "rules of engagement" with partner organizations to guide day-to-day interactions.

COZINESS AND DEPENDENCE

The partners can also get too *cozy* with each other, reaching a comfort level that eliminates consideration of alternative courses of action. This is often linked with a feeling of dependence because no fallback arrangements exist. Quite in contrast, it is a sign of a healthy partnering relationship that partners have discussed, developed, and established contingency plans. These plans protect the legitimate interests of one partner should the other fail to fulfill its commitments due to circumstances beyond its control (*force majeure* or *Act of God*).

CLOUDED JUDGMENT

An arm's-length relationship that becomes a personal friendship can *cloud judgment.* Although it is desirable to develop smooth working relationships based on trust and mutual respect, partners may cross a fine line if a business relationship becomes a personal one. Companies try to avoid such potential problems by fostering team interaction and rotating the individuals involved from time to time.

VULNERABILITY

A strategic partnering relationship can become highly *vulnerable* if it turns into an exclusive long-term linkage that is exempt from the challenges of the marketplace. The relationship may well become sterile if it shuts itself off from the stream of new ideas that a dynamic, competitive marketplace generates. There is a danger of becoming too inwardly focused and ignoring or discounting signs of change. Virtual corporations overcome this danger by being market-sensitive and fleetfooted, and by continuously reconfiguring their networks as market conditions shift.

SLOPPINESS

There is, of course, no excuse for plain *sloppiness,* which can arise from the perspective that "familiarity breeds contempt." It is clearly time for a significant change when the inputs partners receive from each other consistently suffer from unacceptable deficiencies. In fact, it is continuous improvement that is the hallmark of strategic partnering.

SWITCHING COSTS

A final potential drawback derives from the *costs of altering existing arrangements.* Where organizations have established extensive systems and operational linkages, terminating an existing relationship and switching to a new partner or going it alone can be quite costly and time consuming .

Eastern States Bankcard Association was a not-for-profit organization owned by its 300 member banks. It essentially served as the outsourced credit card department for its members, issuing cards and monthly statements, and processing charges and payments in their names. The departure of a bank from this group represented a loss in processing volume, and thus a reduction in the economies of scale. Therefore, the association formally imposed a *resignation assessment* on the departing member to compensate the remaining members for the loss in volume.

It would be shortsighted and dangerous to downplay or ignore the potential risks inherent in strategic partnering. Properly understood and managed, though, these risks become opportunities to beat the odds and profit immensely from the leverage of partnering.

Benefits of Partnering

Although companies must acknowledge and proactively manage the potential risks, strategic partnering with carefully selected and developed partners brings impressive benefits that outweigh the risks. Below is a representative list of these benefits.

Benefits of Partnering

- Quality
- Competitiveness
- Momentum
- Peace of mind

- Innovation
- Profitability
- Dynamics
- Synergy

QUALITY

Strategic partnering results not only in the achievement of consistent *quality*, but also in its continuous joint improvement for the mutual benefit of the partners and the organizations with whom they do business. So it has a ripple effect beyond the immediate players that is recognized in the criteria for the Malcolm Baldrige National Quality Award. The Baldrige Award emphasizes customer-driven quality, customer-supplier interaction and linkages, and customer satisfaction. It is no surprise, then, that Baldrige winner Motorola urges its suppliers to apply for the award, and that Ames Rubber, a Xerox supplier, has followed its big customer into the Winner's Circle.

Xerox is also among the companies who annually publish full-page thank-you notes in *The Wall Street Journal*, acknowledging its certified suppliers for their contributions to its performance and its ability to win quality awards around the world. As befits a global company, these suppliers hail from all continents. To be certified by a customer like Xerox, suppliers must demonstrate zero-defect, on-time deliveries and continuous improvement for an extended period, thus obviating the need for incoming inspection.

INNOVATION

Strategic partnering also generates powerful forces for joint *innovation*. It is natural for partnered corporations to share their new product plans with each other and engage in joint development efforts to save both time and money. User-driven innovation and early supplier involvement in new product initiatives are typical and highly beneficial manifestations of partnering. Shared financing of the often substantial investments in new materials, technologies, and products, and joint ownership of patents frequently grow out of such fertile relationships.

COMPETITIVENESS

The close cooperation of strategic partnering bears rich fruit in the form of increased *competitiveness* of the partners. As they analyze the process of their joint value creation and streamline it for maximum responsiveness and efficiency, they inevitably reduce cycle time and cost. This puts them in "fighting trim" for the global competitive race. They can bring resources to bear that are not available to their competitors who are going it alone. And their alliance is not easily duplicated by others who may try to imitate but will find it difficult to replicate smooth functioning operational linkages and close working relationships.

PROFITABILITY, MOMENTUM, AND DYNAMICS

Partners feel the payoff on the bottom line. As they cut waste and trade the tedium of competitive sourcing and marketing processes for the power of long-term relationships, their *profitability* improves drastically and lastingly. They confidently invest to improve performance and produce remarkable returns. This creates a strong *momentum* of growth or bandwagon effect. As the whole of the partnering relationship is greater than the sum of its parts, the "good times roll." The secret, though, is to keep the relationship from going stale. The partners must be committed to continuous improvement to remain at the leading edge of their industries. This relentless quest for improvement results in a steadily evolving or *dynamic alliance*.

PEACE OF MIND AND SYNERGY

An immeasurable outcome of working closely with reliable and trusted partners is *peace of mind*. It is immensely beneficial to know that the partner has one's own interests at heart and will come through in any situation. The mutuality and exclusiveness of the alliance involve so strong a bond that total support is a given. As the partners feed and participate in each other's single and joint initiatives, their cooperation sparks a powerful *synergy*. They leverage off each other's strengths and create an unbeatable combination.

3

MAKING PARTNERING WORK

As attractive and necessary as strategic partnering is, the real challenge is to succeed at it over the long run with a substantial number of partners. So it is helpful to learn from the experiences of others in overcoming obstacles and avoiding pitfalls. This enables prospective partners to reduce their cycle time successfully and enjoy the rewards of partnering earlier and longer at a lower cost in wear and tear.

OVERCOMING OBSTACLES

For most managers and corporations, partnering is anything but a natural activity. Individuals and organizations are where they are because they look out for themselves. They rely on their own abilities, resources, and endeavors, and are inwardly focused on "doing their own thing." They typically pride themselves on their individualism and achievements in the face of adversity, and feel that they are doing just fine and don't need any help.

So advocates of partnering face some real challenges in spreading the gospel and making it a way of life. The list below shows a number of key challenges.

Obstacles to Partnering

- Resistance to change
- Short-term thinking
- Cultural differences
- Self-interest
- Turfism

Resistance to Change

The most basic obstacle to strategic partnering is *resistance to change*. Continuing a familiar routine is very comfortable. The discomfort of having to give it up and try something new and different is often palpable. In our turbulent world of impermanence, change seems to attack established patterns all too frequently. In the daily battle to preserve tradition against the relentless onslaught of what appears to be change for the sake of change, digging in and fighting the erosion of the familiar is all too natural.

Short-term Thinking

Another major obstacle is *short-term thinking*. In the United States, Wall Street analysts often display an attitude of "what have you done for me lately?" Stock values can tumble and executives can lose their jobs whenever corporate profits dip below prior levels. Consequently, most are impatient with the time-consuming process of building relationships. Instead, many are inclined to go for the "quick fix" or "low-hanging fruit" at the expense of initiatives with longer-term paybacks. In contrast, in Japan, a strong set of intercorporate ties within corporate "families" (*keiretsu*) represents "patient capital" that supports worthwhile initiatives over extended periods of time, regardless of short-term results.

Cultural Differences

A third significant obstacle to strategic partnering can arise in the *cultural differences* between the would-be corporate partners. *Culture* refers to an organization's values and behaviors. One end of the spectrum is rigid bureaucracy; the other is the freewheeling entrepreneurial culture. These extremes blend with each other like oil and water and are unlikely to result in lasting alliances. Although cultural change is possible and often necessary, it is usually slow and painful in coming and can hardly be counted on to make partnering succeed.

Self-Interest

A fourth obstacle is an organization's unenlightened emphasis on its own *self-interest*. Looking out for number one is hardly a prescription for a successful, budding partnering effort. It leaves little room for consideration of the other party's legitimate interests. Those who regard business only as an adversarial situation advocate this kind of approach. They tend to view negotiation as a game and develop strategies and tactics for gaining advantage. In contrast, the Harvard Negotiation Project promotes a perspective of mutual gains that encourages solutions beneficial to both parties and their relationship.

Turfism

A final impediment to strategic partnering arises from narrow-minded thinking that operates at the functional level. *Turfism* is behavior that aims to protect a function's turf against unwelcome intrusions and change. It cherishes existing prerogatives and "splendid isolation." It resents cooperation and teamwork because they could diminish its power and expose its weaknesses. Turfism involves thinking in terms of departments, not processes; in terms of problems, not opportunities; and in terms of preserving the status quo, not redesigning responsibilities for maximum leverage.

Preparation for Partnering

To the extent that these obstacles exist and shape an organization's actions, it is advisable to initiate a process of introspection and corporate renewal before moving into partnering. The stage clearly must be set before partnering can become a reality. There must be a realization that the old (that is, current) way of doing business is inadequate in a world of intense competition and turbulent change. There must be a comprehensive reexamination of business processes to flush out inefficiencies. Everyone must fully agree that it is in their best interest for the organization to concentrate on what it does best—its core competencies. The corporation must leverage these unique capabilities by alliances with complementary partners. Unless these insights, attitudes, and processes are well established, strategic partnering is not likely to be successful. Instead, it may well backfire by demoralizing the troops and diminishing profitability and market share. So an organization must first put its house in order before it can meaningfully and successfully reach out and team up with partners for maximum mutual benefit.

ESSENTIALS OF SUCCESSFUL PARTNERING

To unleash the tremendous power of strategic partnering, an organization merely needs to adhere to a few common-sense guidelines. Below is a list of these.

Partnering Power Tools

- Continuous improvement
- Long-term commitment
- Empowerment
- Common values
- Leadership

Continuous Improvement

Strategic partnering unfolds its true potential as the partners engage in a process of *continuous improvement*. This process benefits greatly from mutual input and feedback in the form of a report card. This powerful tool is presented in Figure 9.

EVALUATING EXPECTATIONS AND REQUIREMENTS

It is essential that the partners clearly communicate their expectations and requirements to each other. They are listed in column A of the report card under the heading *Dimensions*. To help the other partner prioritize these requirements, column B shows their weight. Their relative importance is indicated by allocating 100 percent among them. Column C shows the

THE CONTINUOUS IMPROVEMENT REPORT CARD

Report Card

A	B	C	D	
DIMENSIONS	IMPOR-TANCE (%)	PERFORMANCE RATINGS	WEIGHTED RATINGS (= B x C)	5 = Excellent 4 = Very good 3 = Good 2 = Fair 1 = Poor
	100%	OVERALL SCORE		

Figure 9. The Continuous Improvement Report Card

numerical evaluation that one partner assigns to the other partner's performance according to the scale along the side of Figure 9.

To compute weighted ratings, multiply columns B and C and enter the result in column D. Weighted ratings take into account not only the specific performance rating, but also its importance to the other partner as expressed in column B. The overall score on a given report card, then, is the sum of the weighted ratings. The maximum overall score is 500. The actual overall score, as compared with this maximum, measures relative performance over time and helps identify opportunities for improvement.

STAYING COMPETITIVE

Commitment to continuous improvement means that the partners will never be satisfied with the status quo. They set ambitious goals for their joint effort and measure actual performance against them. But they do not stop there because doing so could leave them dangerously out of touch with the reality of the marketplace and too strongly focused internally. This danger is illustrated by the experience of American automobile manufacturers as they moved into the '90s. The good news was that the quality of their vehicles was improving. The bad news was that the quality of the cars made by their Japanese competitors was improving faster. This meant that they were actually falling behind in the competitive quality race while making progress toward their own internal goals.

BENCHMARKING

It is essential for any partnering relationship to continually run a reality check by comparing the partners' achievements against those of their fiercest competitors and, ultimately, against the best performers in the world. This ongoing comparison is known as *benchmarking*. As the Baldrige criteria highlight, this process is the cornerstone of world-class quality. Performance improvements tend to come in small doses, as incremental achievements rather than quantum leaps. They continue to happen only if they are based on organization-wide involvement, teamwork, and a spirit that seeks to outperform anybody else.

Long-Term Commitment

The second power tool of partnering is *long-term commitment*. It is intimately linked with the first: Continuous improvement requires long-term commitment. Only partners who are firmly committed to each other and in it for the long haul will provide the resources and produce the results that are necessary for the success of their partnering effort. This commitment has to be organization-wide, but must be particularly strong at the executive level. Unanticipated delays, setbacks, and costs plague many a cooperative effort at the outset as the partners get to know and work with each other. Asking for the quick fix and being swayed by short-term results that fall short of ambitious goals or expectations are sure-fire ways to destroy a budding relationship before it gets a chance to flourish and prove itself. Long-term commitment requires the allocation of adequate resources and patient investment for the long haul. It requires abundant faith in the merits of the cause and the promising future of the joint endeavor. Japanese firms demonstrate this kind of unrelenting faith in and support for their partners in their relationships.

Empowerment

A third power tool for strategic partnering is *empowerment*. It involves granting key players the power to apply their talents and judgment and do what is right in a given situation, unencumbered by bureaucratic rules and procedures. Empowerment goes a long way toward making strategic partnering work by enabling each party's representatives to act in a way that serves both partners' long-term interests, regardless of short-term costs.

Common Values

An essential prerequisite for success, though, is that partners agree on a *common set of values*. As core elements of corporate culture, values are powerful forces that drive corporate and individual behavior. They represent firmly held beliefs that form the underpinnings of an organization's strategic vision or future direction. Understandably, a cooperative effort is greatly enhanced when the partners' values coincide. Such values may include a commitment to quality, innovation, openness, flexibility, diversity of talent, dignity of the individual, and respect for the environment. Inasmuch as values govern behavior, commonly held values facilitate agreement and joint action.

Leadership

Last, but certainly not least, successful strategic partnering is built on *leadership*. Leadership involves formulating a strategic vision and rallying others in pursuit of this dream. It also requires providing adequate resources and support to enable qualified people to carry out appropriate actions that enhance the relationship and its success.

4

CONCLUSION

Strategic partnering is the wave of the future because it leverages the core competencies of an organization by joining forces with complementary partners. It applies the concept of teamwork across organizational boundaries. It reengineers the process of value creation to improve the relationship between the function and cost of a product. Properly managed and implemented, strategic partnering is a powerful force for productive change and the mutual benefit of the partners. Resourceful leaders follow the 12-step partnering process described in section 2 to bring these benefits to their organizations.

FOR FURTHER READING

Bhote, Keki R. *Strategic Supply Management: A Blueprint for Revitalizing the Manufacturer-Supplier Partnership*. New York: AMACOM, 1989.

Burt, David N. and Michael F. Doyle. *The American Keiretsu: A Strategic Weapon for Global Competitiveness*. Homewood, Ill: Business One Irwin, 1993.

Byrne, John A. "The Virtual Corporation," *Business Week* (February 8, 1993): 98-102.

Hale, Roger L., Ronald E. Kowal, Donald D. Carlton, and Tim K. Sehnert. *Made in the USA: How One American Company Helps Satisfy Customer Needs Through Strategic Supplier Quality Management*. Minneapolis: Tennant Company, 1991.

Lewis, Jordan D. *Partnerships for Profit*. New York: Free Press, 1990.

Magnet, Myron. "The New Golden Rule of Business," *Fortune*, February 21, 1994: 60-64.

Monczka, Robert M. and Robert J. Trent. *Cross-Functional Sourcing Team Effectiveness*. Tempe, Ariz.: Center for Advanced Purchasing Studies, 1993.

Senge, Peter M. *The Fifth Discipline: The Art and Practice of the Learning Organization*. New York: Doubleday, 1990.

ABOUT THE AUTHOR

Eberhard E. Scheuing is professor of marketing, director of the Business Research Institute, and director of Continuing Management Education at St. John's University in New York. Born and educated in Germany, he received his M.B.A. in management and his Ph.D. in marketing from the University of Munich.

The author of 22 books and more than 500 articles, Dr. Scheuing is the founder and president of the International Service Quality Association and a frequent seminar leader, conference speaker, and consultant.

The Management Master Series

The *Management Master Series* offers business managers leading-edge information on the best contemporary management practices. Written by highly respected authorities, each short "briefcase book" addresses a specific topic in a concise, to-the-point presentation, using both text and illustrations. These are ideal books for busy managers who want to get the whole message quickly.

Set 1 — Great Management Ideas

1. *Management Alert: Don't Reform—Transform!*
   Michael J. Kami

   Transform your corporation: adapt faster, be more productive, perform better.

2. *Vision, Mission, Total Quality: Leadership Tools for Turbulent Times*
   William F. Christopher
   Build your vision and mission to achieve world class goals.

3. *The Power of Strategic Partnering*
   Eberhard E. Scheuing
   Take advantage of the strengths in your customer-supplier chain.

4. *New Performance Measures*
   Brian H. Maskell
   Measure service, quality, and flexibility with methods that address your customers' needs.

5. *Motivating Superior Performance*
   Saul W. Gellerman
   Use these key factors—nonmonetary as well as monetary—to improve employee performance.

6. *Doing and Rewarding: Inside a High-Performance Organization*
   Carl G. Thor
   Design systems to reward superior performance and encourage productivity.

PRODUCTIVITY PRESS, Dept. BK, PO Box 13390, Portland, OR 97213-0390
Telephone: 1-800-394-6868   Fax: 1-800-394-6286

Set 2 — Total Quality

7. *The 16-Point Strategy for Productivity and Total Quality*
   William F. Christopher and Carl G. Thor

   Essential points you need to know to improve the performance of your organization.

8. *The TQM Paradigm: Key Ideas That Make It Work*
   Derm Barrett

   Get a firm grasp of the world-changing ideas behind the Total Quality movement.

9. *Process Management: A Systems Approach to Total Quality*
   Eugene H. Melan

   Learn how a business process orientation will clarify and streamline your organization's capabilities.

10. *Practical Benchmarking for Mutual Improvement*
    Carl G. Thor

    Discover a down-to-earth approach to benchmarking and building useful partnerships for quality.

11. *Mistake-Proofing: Designing Errors Out*
    Richard B. Chase and Douglas M. Stewart

    Learn how to eliminate errors and defects at the source with inexpensive poka-yoke devices and staff creativity.

12. *Communicating, Training, and Developing for Quality Performance*
    Saul W. Gellerman

    Gain quick expertise in communication and employee development basics.

These books are sold in sets. Each set is $85.00 plus $5.00 shipping and handling. Future sets will cover such topics as Customer Service, Leadership, and Innovation. For complete details, call 800-394-6868 or fax 800-394-6286.

PRODUCTIVITY PRESS, Dept. BK, PO Box 13390, Portland, OR 97213-0390
Telephone: 1-800-394-6868   Fax: 1-800-394-6286

BOOKS FROM PRODUCTIVITY PRESS

Productivity Press provides individuals and companies with materials they need to achieve excellence in quality, productivity and the creative involvement of all employees. Through sets of learning tools and techniques, Productivity supports continuous improvement as a vision, and as a strategy. Many of our leading-edge products are direct source materials translated into English for the first time from industrial leaders around the world. Call toll-free 1-800-394-6868 for our free catalog.

Handbook for Productivity Measurement and Improvement
William F. Christopher and Carl G. Thor, eds.
An unparalleled resource! In over 100 chapters, nearly 80 front-runners in the quality movement reveal the evolving theory and specific practices of world-class organizations. Spanning a wide variety of industries and business sectors, they discuss quality and productivity in manufacturing, service industries, profit centers, administration, nonprofit and government institutions, health care and education. Contributors include Robert C. Camp, Peter F. Drucker, Jay W. Forrester, Joseph M. Juran, Robert S. Kaplan, John W. Kendrick, Yasuhiro Monden, and Lester C. Thurow. Comprehensive in scope and organized for easy reference, this compendium belongs in every company and academic institution concerned with business and industrial viability.
ISBN 1-56327-007-2 / 1344 pages / $90.00 / Order HPM-B235

The Benchmarking Management Guide
American Productivity & Quality Center
If you're planning, organizing, or actually undertaking a benchmarking program, you need the most authoritative source of information to help you get started and to manage the process all the way through. Written expressly for managers of benchmarking projects by the APQC's renowned International Benchmarking Clearinghouse, this guide provides exclusive information from members who have already paved the way. It includes information on training courses and ways to apply Baldrige, Deming, and ISO 9000 criteria for internal assessment, and has a complete bibliography of benchmarking literature.
ISBN 1-56327-045-5 / 260 pages / $40.00 / Order BMG-B235

Fast Focus on TQM
A Concise Guide to Companywide Learning
Derm Barrett
Finally, here's one source for all your TQM questions. Compiled in this concise, easy-to-read handbook are definitions and detailed explanations of over 160 key terms used in TQM. Organized in a simple alphabetical glossary form, the book can be used either as a primer for anyone being introduced to TQM or as a complete reference guide. It helps to align teams, departments, or entire organizations in a common understanding and use of TQM terminology. For anyone entering or currently involved in TQM, this is one resource you must have.
ISBN 1-56327-049-8 / 186 pages / $20.00 / Order FAST-B235

The Teamwork Advantage
An Inside Look at Japanese Product and Technology Development
Jeffrey L. Funk
How are so many Japanese manufacturing firms shortening product time-to-market, reducing costs, and improving quality? The answer is teamwork. Dr. Funk spent 18 months as a visiting engineer at Mitsubishi and Yokogawa Hokushin Electric and knows firsthand how Japanese corporate culture promotes effective teamwork in production, design, and technology development. Here's a penetrating case study and analysis that presents a truly viable model for the West.
ISBN 0-915299-69-0 / 508 pages / $50.00 / Order TEAMAD-B235

PRODUCTIVITY PRESS, Dept. BK, PO Box 13390, Portland, OR 97213-0390
Telephone: 1-800-394-6868   Fax: 1-800-394-6286

TO ORDER: Write, phone, or fax Productivity Press, Dept. BK, P.O. Box 13390, Portland, OR 97213-0390, phone 1-800-394-6868, fax 1-800-394- 6286. Send check or charge to your credit card (American Express, Visa, MasterCard accepted).

U.S. ORDERS: Add $5 shipping for first book, $2 each additional for UPS surface delivery. Add $5 for each AV program containing 1 or 2 tapes; add $12 for each AV program containing 3 or more tapes. We offer attractive quantity discounts for bulk purchases of individual titles; call for more information.

INTERNATIONAL ORDERS: Write, phone, or fax for quote and indicate shipping method desired. For international callers, telephone number is 503-235-0600 and fax number is 503-235-0909. Prepayment in U.S. dollars must accompany your order (checks must be drawn on U.S. banks). When quote is returned with payment, your order will be shipped promptly by the method requested.

NOTE: Prices are in U.S. dollars and are subject to change without notice.